DICTIONARY
OF
WITCHCRAFT

DICTIONARY OF WITCHCRAFT

COLLIN DE PLANCY

Edited and translated by
Wade Baskin

PHILOSOPHICAL LIBRARY, INC.
New York

Distributed to the Trade by
BOOK SALES, INC.
352 Park Avenue South
New York 10, N.Y.

ISBN 978-0-8065-2976-9

Copyright MXMLXV by Philosophical Library, Inc., 15 East 40th Street, New York, N.Y. 10016. Library of Congress Catalog Card No. 65-11952. Originally published under the title *Dictionary of Demonology*. Manufactured in the United States of America. All rights reserved.

TRANSLATOR'S INTRODUCTION

According to Stendhal's definition of Romanticism as anything written to please contemporaries, Jacques-Albin-Simon Collin de Plancy (1793-1887) should be numbered among the great writers of this age. His aim in the *Dictionary of Demonology* was to draw together, following the pattern set earlier by the Encyclopedists, a vast amount of material that would interest, entertain and instruct others. The surest measure of his success is the fact that readers exhausted edition after edition of his work.

Collin de Plancy's predilection for the irrational, the harrowing and the pathetic gives him a place in the genesis of one phase of Romanticism. His *Dictionary* was consulted by some of the greatest Romantic writers, notably by Hugo. His passion for the darker side of the human consciousness also serves as a common link between him and his better known contemporary, Charles Nodier, who is generally credited with having enlarged the literary horizon of the Romantic writers by focusing attention on the occult. Less direct but no less obvious is his kinship with German writers like Novalis, Hoffmann, Tieck and Goethe and with the English practitioners of the Gothic, particularly "Monk" Lewis.

The title of the work is aptly chosen. Collin de Plancy knew his abilities and he knew his public. Even as the Age of Enlightenment was giving way to the Age of Positivism, stories of witchcraft, terrifying ghosts and monstrous events were meeting with popular success. With his passion for strange stories, legends and customs, and his facility for compiling and editing information, Collin de Plancy was ideally suited to the task of bringing out just such a book.

His career as a writer, or more appropriately, as a polygraph, had admirably prepared him for his task. He had worked as a printer and bookseller in the town of Plancy and in Paris. A facile writer ever mindful of popular tastes, he managed to earn a comfortable living by practicing his craft under a variety of pseudonyms — C. Brindamour, Dr. Ensenada, Hormisdas Peath, Jacques de l'Enclos, Jean de Septchênes, to cite but a few of them. Alert to the development of every new trend, he flooded the market with his books. On the subject of superstition, for instance, he published some eighty volumes.

Pseudo-science was his mainstay. He wrote, generally under names other than his own up until the time he published his *Dictionary,* on cartomancy, chiromancy, divination, folklore, magic, alchemy and a host of related topics. Most significant, however, was the appearance of three volumes compiled between 1819 and 1825.

In 1819, under the name of Gabrielle de P . . . (probably his wife or his cousin), he published his *History of Phantoms and Demons That Have Appeared to Men.* The following year he published a work calculated to please everyone interested in the irrational. It was titled *Dictionary of Madness and Reason,* and it dealt with fakirs, alchemists, magicians and ghosts. Five years later he compiled and published an extremely popular work titled *The Devil's Self-Portrait, or a Collection of Short Stories and Tales about the Adventures and the Character of Demons, Their Machinations, Their Misfortunes, Their Love Affairs, and the Services That They Have Been Able to Render to Men.*

Having discovered the road to popular success early in his career, Collin de Plancy knew in advance that by wedding his dictionary and his demons, he would produce his most successful work.

The crowning achievement of Romanticism is that it has served as the mother lode for the major literary movements of the past two centuries. Some of those who contributed to the emergence of Romanticism achieved fame, some were forgotten. Collin de Plancy, in spite of the sheer volume of his output, might have been forgotten except for the one work that stands as his enduring monument, the *Dictionary of Demonology.*

WADE BASKIN

Southeastern State College

DICTIONARY OF WITCHCRAFT

Abel de Larue

In the year 1582, Abel de Larue, called "The Smasher," appeared before Nicolas Quatre-Sols, civil and criminal lieutenant in the bailiwick of Coulommiers, charged with having cast a spell on Jean Moureau on the day of his marriage to Phare Fleuriot. . . . After some hesitation, he admitted the charges. He confessed that he had been placed by his mother in the Franciscan monastery, and that he had become enraged at Caillet, the instructor of the novices, who had beaten him. As he was thinking about avenging himself, a black spaniel appeared before him and promised not to hurt him in any way provided he would surrender himself to the dog. The black dog, which was really a demon, took him to a room in the monastery called "The Bookstore" and then disappeared after telling him that he would always come to his rescue. . . . The court sentenced the accused to be hanged and garroted . . . and decreed that the sorcerer's body should be burned after his death. The decree was executed on July 20, 1582.

Abigor

A demon of high degree, the grand duke of hell. Sixty legions are under his command. He reveals himself as a handsome rider bearing a lace, a standard or a scepter. He knows all the secrets of war, foresees the future, and teaches leaders how to win the love of their soldiers.

Abnormal Births

Ambroise Paré cites the case of a Neopolitan pig with the head of a man. Bayle speaks of a woman who gave birth to a black cat, which was burned by the Inquisition as being the offspring of a succubus. . . . All such accounts must be rejected unless attested by sufficient evidence. It is reasonable to assume that one-eyed monsters, such as the Cyclops, have been born, but not that a woman can give birth to an elephant or that one pregnancy can result in the birth of one hundred and fifty children. The most fecund woman on record . . . is a Russian who with the help of four husbands gave birth to sixty-two children during her lifetime.

Abracadabra

A famous mystical word used especially in Persia and in Syria. When written as in the accompanying figure and worn as an amulet around the neck, it was believed to ward off diseases and to be particularly effective in curing a fever.

```
A B R A C A D A B R A
 A B R A C A D A B R
  A B R A C A D A B
   A B R A C A D A
    A B R A C A D
     A B R A C A
      A B R A C
       A B R A
        A B R
         A B
          A
```

Abrasax or Abraxas

A god in certain Asian theogonies. From his name is derived the magical word abracadabra. He is represented on amulets as having the head of a cock, the feet of a dragon, and a whip in his hand. Demonologists have made him a demon with the head of a king and with serpents for his legs. The Egyptian Basilides, second-century heretics, looked upon him as their supreme god. Finding that the seven Greek letters contained in his name amounted to 365, the number of days in the year, they placed at his command several spirits who presided over the three hundred and sixty-five heavens and to whom they attributed three hundred and sixty-five virtues, one for each day. The Basilides also said that Jesus Christ, Our Savior, was but a benevolent spirit sent to the earth by Abrasax. They deviated from the doctrine of their leader.

Adam (the Abbot)

While the Templars were being annihilated in France, the devil appeared before Father Adam in various guises. The evil spirit first appeared as a tree and blocked his passage . . . but the abbot made the sign of the cross and caused it to disappear, leaving in the air the odor of sulfur. He next appeared in the shape of a tall man with a long, skinny neck. The abbot . . . lost his patience, made a circle on the ground, and drew a cross inside the circle. The devil was forced to surrender. He changed his ears into horns, but this did not prevent the abbot from heaping abuse upon him. The devil, offended, returned in the form of a cartwheel and rolled lightly over his belly. . . . Then he allowed the abbot to continue peacefully along his route.

Adrammelech

Grand chancellor of hell, superintendent of the wardrobe of the ruler of demons, and president of the high council of devils. He was worshiped at Sepharvahim, an Assyrian city, where children were burned on altars. The rabbis say that he reveals himself in the shape of a mule, and sometimes in the shape of a peacock.

Aldon

Two Lombard noblemen named Aldon and Granson had displeased Cunibert, the king of Lombardy, and the latter had resolved to have them killed. . . . A big fly alighted on his forehead and gave him a vigorous bite. Cunibert struck the insect but managed to deprive him of but one leg, and the fly disappeared. At the same instant Aldon and Granson, who were together, saw before them a man who seemed exhausted and who had a wooden leg. This man informed them of the king's plan, advised them to flee, and vanished immediately thereafter. The two noblemen gave thanks to the spirit . . . and departed, as the circumstances dictated.

Amduscias

Grand duke of hell. He has the shape of a unicorn, but when called forth he reveals himself in the shape of a man. When commanded to do so, he gives concerts; though he is not seen on such occasions, one hears the sound of trumpets and of other musical instruments. Trees sway to the sound of his voice. He commands twenty-nine legions.

Andras

Grand marquis of hell. He appears to have the body of an angel and the head of a wood owl, and to be riding a black wolf and carrying in his hand a pointed saber. He teaches those whom he favors to kill their enemies, masters and servants. He stirs up trouble and dissension. He commands thirty legions.

Apparitions

"It is by no means rare," said Voltaire, "for a person under strong emotional stress to see something that does not exist." A woman, accused in London in 1726 of being an accomplice to the murder of her husband, denied the fact. She was shown her shroud . . . and her wild imagination made her see her husband. She threw herself at his feet and tried to embrace him. She told the jury that she had seen her husband. . . . Theodoric saw in the head of a fish that had been brought to his table the head of a man whom he had assassinated. Charles IX, after the Massacre of St. Bartholomew, saw blood and dead victims not in dream but in the convulsions of a troubled mind which in vain sought sleep. . . . Apparitions, said Iamblichus, are analogous to their essence; the appearance of the gods (or of the saints) is comforting, that of archangels terrifying, that of angels less frightening, and that of demons revolting. He adds that it is rather difficult to recognize oneself in the apparitions of specters, for they come in thousands of varieties.

Ashes

It was held, during the seventeenth century, that corpses, the ashes of animals and even the ashes of burned plants contained reproductive seeds; that a frog, for example, could engender other frogs even as it decayed, and that the ashes of roses had produced new roses. . . . Peasants believe that a Christian who has eaten seven bushels of ashes is certain to go directly to paradise.

Astaroth

Powerful grand duke in hell. He has the face of an ugly angel and is seen riding on an infernal dragon, holding a viper in his left hand. Some magicians say that he holds sway in the West, that he solicits the friendship of great noblemen, and that he must be summoned on Wednesday. The Sidonians and the Philistians worship him. He is said to be the treasurer in hell. Wierus states that he knows both the past and the future, that he freely answers questions about the most occult matters, and that it is easy to make him talk about creation, the misdeeds and the fall of the angels . . . but that in his conversations he maintains that he himself was unjustly punished. . . . He is cited as one of the seven princes of hell who, according to the English tradition, visited Faust.

Aubry (Nicole)

Nicole Aubry, the wife of a tailor in Vervins, went to her grandfather's tomb to pray. She thought she saw her grandfather, who had died without confessing his sins, come out of his tomb and order her to have masses said for the repose of his soul, which was in purgatory. The young woman was terror-stricken. When her sickness continued unabated, the report circulated that the devil had taken the shape of Vieilliot, her grandfather, and that she was possessed. Claude Lautrichet, a priest, and Guillaume

Lourdet, a teacher, conjured up the spirit, which tried to pass through the soul or the good angel of the deceased, but the spirit's words and actions showed that he was an angel of darkness. . . . Pierre Delamotte, a Dominican friar and a renowned exorcist, made the spirit admit that he was Beelzebub. Prayers, fasting and macerations were prescribed. A monk whipped himself publicly to obtain the expulsion of the demon. In an attempt to exorcise the evil spirit, the possessed woman was given communion, and she ceased to gambol about.

Aneiran (Isaac de)

Sorcerer tried in Bordeaux at the age of twenty-five. Asked how he had learned witchcraft, he admitted that at the age of ten or twelve . . . he had gone one day to a neighbor's house for fire. He was asked . . . by the old woman whether he wanted to see the grand master of sabbats . . . and carried through the air to the place where men and women were shouting and dancing. A big black man came up to him . . . and struck him on the shoulder, saying, "Stay, stay. . . ." Later he saw that the big black man had also marked him just above his hand. Finally, he added, the devil . . . came one day and took him back to the sabbat, where he danced and ate like all the others. He was . . . condemned to be burned on May 8, 1609.

Aupetit (Pierre)

Priest and sorcerer in the village of Fossas, parish of Paias, near the town of Chalu in Limousin, executed as a caster of spells and a practitioner of magic, at the age of fifty, on May, 25, 1598. . . . To extract from him the truth, he was put on the rack. He confessed that he had gone to the sabbat; that he read from the book of spells; that the devil, in the shape of a sheep, more black than white, had the others kiss his behind; that Crapoulet, a notorious sorcerer, had taught him the secret of using levers, of staunching and stopping the flow of blood; that his demon or familiar spirit was named Beelzebub; that he had been given the spirit's little finger . . . that this devil had taught him what he must do to possess any woman or girl of his choosing, and in any manner of his choosing. . . . He persisted with his ridiculous revelations even under torture.

Aymar (Jacques)

Peasant born in Saint-Veran, in the province of Dauphiné, on September 8, 1662, between midnight and one o'clock in the morning. He was a mason and became famous as a result of his use of the divining rod. Some have attributed his rare talent to the precise time of his birth, for his brother, born during the same month two years later, had no success with the divining rod. Previously the rod had been employed only in searching for metals used in alchemy. But Jacques Aymar performed marvels with his rod. He laid claim to the discovery of underground streams, forgotten landmarks, spells, thefts, and assassins. . . . He finally confessed that he was an imposter, that his rod had no power, and that he had tried to enrich himself through his acts of charlatanism.

B

Bael

Demon named in *The Great Book of Spells* as the head of the powers of evil. He is also named first in Wierus' inventory in his famous *Pseudomonarchia doemonum*. Wierus calls Bael the first king in hell; his states are in the eastern part of hell. He has three heads, of which one is shaped like a frog, another like a man, and the third like a cat. His voice is harsh, but he is a good fighter. Those who invoke him are made alert and cunning, and are taught the means of making themselves invisible when necessary. Seventy legions are under his command.

Bayard

Horse belonging to the four sons of Aymon. He had the shape of an ordinary horse when he carried only one of the brothers, and he grew longer when he had to carry all four of them. Many marvels are attributed to this celebrated steed, characterized particularly by his incredible speed.

Bayer

In 1726 Bayer, a priest from the diocese of Constance, was frightened by a specter or evil spirit that appeared in the shape of a badly dressed peasant with a wicked countenance and an unbearable stench. . . . He returned every day around four o'clock in the afternoon, and every night until daybreak. He appeared in various guises, sometimes in the shape of a spaniel, sometimes in the shape of a lion or other terrible animal; at times he appeared in the shape of a man, and often in the shape of a woman or girl, while the priest was at table or in bed, enticing him to commit lewd acts. . . . Finally attempts were made to exorcise the evil spirit, but to no avail. Then on Palm Sunday a branch and a sword that had been blessed were brandished on two different occasions, and after that, the specter disappeared and did not return. The account was attested by a Capuchin friar, who witnessed most of the events, on August 29, 1749.

Beans

Pythagoras prohibited his pupils from eating beans, which he revered especially because they were useful to him in his work with magic and because he was convinced that they were animate. . . . He borrowed his ideas about beans from the Egyptians, who would not touch them. He is said to have preferred death at the hands of his pursuers to safety when the latter entailed crossing a beanfield. . . . The ancients offered black beans to the infernal divinities; they were thought to serve as a refuge for certain souls. In Egypt, along the banks of the Nile, are little stones made like beans; when applied to the nose of a demoniac, they put his demon to flight. Festus holds that there is something ominous about the flower of the bean, and that the fruit closely resembles the gates of hell.

Belphegor

Demon of ingenious discoveries and inventions. He often assumes the shape of a young woman. He distributes wealth. The Moabites, who called him Baalphegor, workshiped him on Mt. Peor. Some rabbis say that he was paid homage on the commode, and that he was offered the filthy remnants from the digestive tract. . . . Selden, quoted by Banier, holds that he was offered human victims whose flesh was eaten by his priests. Wierus observes that the demon Belphegor always has his mouth open

. . . because he was sometimes worshiped in caverns, where offerings were thrown down to him through an opening.

Berbiguier

Alexis-Vincent-Charles Berbiguier, born in Carpentras, is a living author who published in 1821 . . . a work containing this epigraph: "Jesus Christ was sent to the earth by God the Father in order that he might wash away all sins from mankind; I have reason to believe that I am destined to destroy the enemies of the Supreme Being." The author, who called himself "The Scourge of Goblins," might more aptly be named the Don Quijote of Goblins. He begins with a dedication to all emperors, kings, and sovereign princes from all parts of the globe. "Join me," he says, "and let us destroy the influence of demons, sorcerers and goblins who torment the unhappy inhabitants of your states." He adds that he has been tormented by the devil for twenty-three years.

Beyrevra

Indian demon, master of souls that roam through space

after being changed into airy demons. He is said to have huge crooked nails. Brahma insulted a superior god one day, and Beyrevra, whose task it was to punish him, cut off a head with his nail. Brahma, humiliated, begged for pardon and the god Eswara to console him promised that he would receive just as much respect with his four remaining heads as he had previously with five.

Birck (Humbert)

Well known citizen of Oppenheim and inn-keeper who died in November, 1620, a few days before the feast of St. Martin. On Saturday following his last rites, certain noises were heard in the house where he had lived with his first wife. . . . The master of the house, suspecting that it was her brother-in-law, said: "If you are Humbert, tap on the wall three times." Three taps were heard . . . not only on the wall but also at the fountain. When asked why he haunted this house rather than another, he replied that he had to do so because of conjurations and maledictions. . . . When finally his last desires were fulfilled, Humbert de Birck departed forever.

Black Man

The Black Man promises the poor that he will make them rich if they will give themselves over to him. He is, of course, none other than the devil disguised as an ordinary man. . . . Father Abrams relates the following anecdote: A youth of good parentage but meager means met a man dressed in silk . . . but black, hideous, and with a forbidding look. The man asked him where he was going and why he looked so sad. The young man . . . became suspicious of his magnificent promises and studied him more closely. When he saw that the black man's foot was cloven like the foot of an ox, he was terrified. He made the sign of the cross and invoked the name of Jesus. The specter vanished immediately. Three days later the same man reappeared . . . and threw at his feet a purse filled with gold coins. The young man was again horrified by the devil's propositions . . . and made the sign of the cross. When he returned to his parents . . . he put the coins in the fire and discovered that they were made not of gold but of copper.

Bleeding Nun

A ghost that haunted Lindenberg Castle, making it uninhabitable. . . . She was a nun who wore a veil and a blood-stained dress. In one hand was a dagger, and in the other a lighted lamp. . . . A Spanish nun, she had left the convent to live with the lord of the castle. As unfaithful to her lover as she had been to her God, she stabbed him, only to be stabbed in turn by her accomplice, whom she wanted to marry. Her body was left unburied, and her homeless soul had been wandering about for a century. She begged for a little ground for the former and a few prayers for the latter . . . promised both, she disappeared.

Bohemians (Gypsies)

Everyone has heard of the Bohemians and of the vagabond bands scattered throughout Germany, Holland and France. Under the name of Bohemians, Biscayans and Egyptians they engaged in fortune-telling. The Dutch called them *heyden,* that is, heathen, because they looked upon them as people without a religion. Other nations gave them other names for equally erroneous reasons. . . . It would have been more natural to take them at their word and to say that they are a blend of a race of Jews and vagabond Christians. Around the middle of the fourteenth century Europe was ravaged by the plague. . . . The Christians imagined that the Jews had poisoned the wells and fountains. First great numbers of them were burned, then the goods of those who remained were confiscated and they were expelled. . . . Many of the Jews escaped the stake by fleeing into the forests. There they regrouped and, fifty years later, a few dared to emerge from their dens. . . . During a half-century of solitude they had studied divination, particularly the art of telling a person's fortune by inspecting his hand. They assumed that chiromancy would bring them some money. . . . To avoid stating or denying outright their religion, they agreed to say that their forefathers once dwelt in Egypt, which was true.

Bouchey (Marguerite Ragum)

Wife of a mason in Cologne. She lived toward the end of the sixteenth century. She exhibited a puppet which experts identified as an imp. She confessed that her master, Jehan du Cygne, had intrusted the puppet or mandrake to her for a period of three months. . . . She said that when her master went away, he would tell her: "I am turning my beast over to you. Let no one come near you." She related that once when Jehan was away, she failed to give the puppet anything to eat for three days. Upon his return, the puppet gave him a smart slap in the face. . . . The judge had her put to the rack, and later the Parliament of Paris found her guilty of witchcraft.

Boullé (Thomas)

Vicar of Father Picard and like him a sorcer and implicated in the case of Madeleine Bavan. He cast and broke spells, seduced women and girls, and drove a worshiper crazy by spitting on her. He was also accused of having sat on live coals without being burned and of having used magic to fill his penitents with love. . . . He was dragged on a hurdle through the streets of Rouen, forced to make a full apology, and then burned alive on August 22, 1847.

Bourignon (Antoinette)

Famous visionary, born in Lille in 1616, died in 1680. She was so ugly that she was almost put to death at birth as being a monster. . . . But she is said to have inspired great passions, as some women like her manage to do by developing arresting qualities that make others overlook their ugliness. She was almost stoned to death as a sorceress, however, in Strasbourg. Antoinette Bourignon was very intelligent. Her numerous works, which were all printed at her direction in French, Flemish and German, argued against any external form of worship or liturgy and in favor of mystical perfection.

Brinvilliers (Marie Marguerite de)

Pretty young woman who, from 1666 to 1672 poisoned, without malice and often even with disinterest, parents, friends and servants. She even went into hospitals and administered poison to the patients. All her crimes must be attributed to a horrible type of insanity or to the most atrocious kind of depravity, but not to the devil, as is frequently the case. It is true that Brinvilliers began her criminal career at the age of seven and that superstitious minds feared from the outset that a hideous devil had possessed her. . . . Twenty-four hours after she had been burned at the stake in 1676, the people searched for her bones and treated them as relics, saying that she was a saint . . . for the poisonings continued after her death.

Broomsticks

The idiots who imagined that sorcerers and demons celebrated the sabbat also argued that witches traveled to the sabbat on broomsticks. Nowadays everyone knows that there are no sorcerers and that no one rides on a broomstick.

Butter Crock

A skilled exorcist had sealed several demons in a butter crock. After his death, the demons made a noise in their crock, and the heirs broke it, convinced that they would find something valuable inside. But all they found was an unhappy devil. Away he flew with his companions, leaving the crock empty.

C

Cali

Queen of demons and sultaness. She was completely black and wore a necklace fashioned from golden skulls. In times past she was offered human victims.

Candle

Cardan maintains that to learn whether a treasure is buried in a certain spot . . . a big candle made of human fat must be nailed to a crescent-shaped branch of hazel in such a way as to form a three-pronged fork. If the candle crackles and makes loud noises when lighted, this is a sign that treasure is buried underneath. The closer the candle is placed to the treasure, the more it will crackle, and it will go out when placed beside the treasure. . . . Candles have multiple uses. Occult writers all state that witches, at the sabbat, approach the devil with candles in their hands when they are to kiss his bottom.

Capuchin

The Abbot of Voisenon dreaded the sight of a Capuchin, for he thought that something bad would happen afterwards. One day when he was hunting in a good game preserve, he had the bad fortune to catch sight of a Capuchin. From that moment on, he could not shoot accurately a single time, and to his companions who were making fun of him he said: "Really, men, you have no reason to be nervous; you have never come across a Capuchin."

Caradoc

Holy man who had retired to a small island in the north to live a solitary life. The devil came to offer him his services . . . but Caradoc told him: "I have no need of you or your services." The devil finally departed, angered because he had been offered only insults in exchange for his services. . . .

Carrouge (Jean)

Knight, vassal of Peter the Nobleman, Count of Alençon. He had married a pretty young lady. Obliged to undertake a voyage, he left his wife in his castle, where she showed good judgment. "Now it happened," says Froissard, "that the devil entered the body of Jacques Legris, another vassal of the count, and incited in him the perverse temptation to seduce the knight's wife." One day . . . he took the lady in his arms and satisfied his desires. . . . He paid for the crime with his honor and his blood.

Castalin (Diego)

Three Spaniards, accompanied by a woman who was also a witch and a sorceress, were borne through the clouds by devils from town to town, sometimes traveling a hundred leagues in one day. . . . When questioned, they admitted everything, and went so far as to say that they had made fruit rot wherever they pleased, that they had brought about the death of people and animals, and that they had resolved to do mischief in Bordeaux. . . . The court sentenced Diego Castalin, Francisco Ferdillo, Vincentio Torrados and Catalina Fiosela to be put to the stake and burned alive, along with their books, parchments and other things associated with their magic.

Cataldo

Bishop of Taranto during the sixth century. A thousand years after his death, he appeared one night in a vision to a young Tarantine who had given his life to God and ordered him to dig at a spot which he had pointed out to him, where he had hidden a book written by his hand while he was still alive. . . . The child related his vision to everyone. The people excitedly gathered together and accompanied the child to the spot indicated. They arrived, dug into the ground, and found a small lead casket so tightly sealed that no air could enter it. In the bottom of the casket was the book containing an account of all the troubles and curses that were to befall the kingdom of Naples, King Ferdinand, and his children.

Catherine

A girl died in Peru at the age of sixteen without having received the last sacraments. She was guilty of several acts of sacrilege. Her body, immediately after her death, was found to be so foul that it had to be placed outside the house. . . . At the same time the barking of dogs was heard, and a horse that had formerly been quite gentle began to kick, to thrash about, to break his reins. A young man who was asleep was jerked by the arm and thrown out of his bed. A servant was kicked on her shoulder but was unable to see her attacker; she bore the signs for several weeks. All this happened before Catherine's body was inhumed, proving that her spirit was truly damned. Instead of driving it away through masses, the people had recourse to exorcism.

Caym

Demon belonging to a higher order, grand master of hell. He generally reveals himself as a blackbird. When he appears in human shape . . . he carries a tapered saber. He is said to be the cleverest sophist in hell and can, through the astuteness of his arguments, make the most skilled logician despair. Luther had a famous encounter with Caym and has provided us with the details. Caym understands the songs of birds, the bellowing of oxen, the barking of dogs and the sound of the waves. He knows the future. At times he has revealed himself as a man adorned by a tuft and a peacock's tail. This demon, who was once numbered among the angels, has at his command thirty legions in hell.

Cayol

Landowner in Marseille who died a few years ago. One of his tenants brought him twelve hundred francs one day. He was busy and promised to give the tenant a receipt the following day. The farmer was not in the least disturbed and waited several days to return for the receipt. Cayol had just died of a heart attack. His son took possession of his property. He asked the farmer for the twelve hundred francs already paid, refused to believe the latter's statement, and brought suit against him. . . . Cayol appeared by night and censured his son for his conduct. "Look behind the mirror . . . and you will find my receipt," he said. The young man arose, trembling, found the receipt, and quickly reimbursed the poor farmer for all the expenses he had caused him.

Cecilia

Toward the middle of the sixth century a woman named Cecilia attracted attention in Lisbon. She possessed the art of modulating her voice in such a way as to make it appear to issue at times from her elbow, at times from her foot, at times from a place which it would be improper to name. She engaged in conversation with an invisible being . . . who answered all her questions. The woman was a reputed witch and was possessed by the devil; however, as a special favor, instead of being burned at the stake, she was merely banished forever to the island of St. Thomas, where she died peacefully.

Chapel of the Damned

Raymond Diocres, canon of Notre-Dame in Paris, died in an aura of saintliness in 1084. After his body had been carried into the chancel, he raised his head from the coffin. . . . Those who witnessed the episode were frightened and postponed the service until the next day. Meantime the canon's body was placed in the chapel, which has since been named "The Chapel of the Damned" . . . for during the service the next day, the dead man again spoke out, saying: "I have been damned by the righteous judgment of God." Whereupon, according to the chroniclers, his body was thrown into the sewer.

Charlatans

In times past what was merely the work of charlatans was attributed to the devil or to sorcerers. If we still followed the sixteenth-century pattern of thinking, all of our swindlers would be called sorcerers. . . . There have been all types of charlatans. In 1728, in the time of Law, the most famous of all charlatans, another charlatan named Villars told his friends that his uncle had given him the secret for obtaining water which could prolong life . . . but it was finally discovered that Villars' water was simply spring water, and he was deserted in favor of other charlatans.

Charms

A powerful charm can accomplish anything. Delrio cites a sorcerer who by lighting a certain magic lantern was able to induce all the women in the room to disrobe and dance for him. . . . Most charms are effected through words spoken or written down. Pliny says that in his time charms were used to extinguish fires, to stop the flow of blood from wounds, to set broken bones, to heal gout, to prevent chariots from overturning, etc. The ancients all believed firmly in charms; the formulas used generally consisted of Greek or Latin verses. . . . To ward off sword thrusts or any other form of attack, these words were used: *Sanguis Christi* + *sit inter* + *te* + *et me*.

Chassen (Nicolas)

A little sorcerer from Franeker. During the seventeenth century, at the age of sixteen, he became famous. At school he made strange faces, rolled his eyes and twisted his whole body. He showed his comrades ripe cherries in the dead of winter; then, after offering them to his friends, he took the cherries back and ate them himself. In church, where all the boys sat by themselves, he made money pour from his bench. . . . When asked what he did to produce cherries and money, he replied that a spirit provided them. "Who is this spirit?" he was asked. He replied, winking and then looking straight ahead as if ashamed: "Beelzebub." He added that the devil often appeared to him in the shape of a woman, sometimes in the hideous shape of a goat or a calf, and also sometimes in the shape of a man, but that he always had a deformed leg.

Clairon

Also known as Hippolyte. One of the greatest tragedians of the French stage, she died in 1803. Raucourt relates the tale of a ghost presumed to be the soul of one of her rejected suitors whose passion for her had finally brought about his death. For several months following his death, piercing screams were heard around eleven o'clock every evening . . . and these were later replaced by the sound of pistol shots which, though they struck the window, did no damage. The shots were followed by hand-clapping and then by melodious sounds. After a little more than two years and a half, all such disturbances ceased.

Colas (Antide)

Sixteenth-century witch who, strongly suspected of carnal intercourse with Satan, was visited by Nicolas Millière of Régnancourt, a surgeon, who examined a hole below her navel and made her confess that the devil (whom she

called Lizabet) knew her carnally through this hole. . . .
She confessed that the devil lay down beside her and,
since she would not do as he asked, made her twitch and
tremble, and pricked her left side. Convinced that she was
a witch, the woman was burned at Dôle in 1599.

Collin de Plancy (Jacques)

Author of this dictionary, of which the first edition appeared in two volumes in 1818. He has also published *The Devil's Self-Portrait, The History of Vampires* . . . and several other pseudonymous works. All these works are contained in this second edition of the *Dictionary of Demonology*.

Copulation

Vulgar word signifying the union of the sexes. Demonographers often use it; they say that witches and wizards copulate with the devil at the sabbat. Philo the Jew . . . states that the serpent's temptation of woman signifies allegorically lust which creeps along on its belly. Agrippa and other investigators have said exactly the same thing. . . . The forbidden tree was nothing other than Eve; Adam should have been satisfied with the other fruits in the garden of sensuous pleasures, that is, all the forms of beauty represented by the sylphs, nymphs and other daughters of the elements; and he should have allowed Eve to enjoy the salamanders, male sylphs and gnomes, who could have won her love. Then no heroes would have been born, and the earth would have been populated by wondrous people exhibiting strength and wisdom. . . . Noah allowed his wife to be seduced by the salamander Oromasis, prince of fiery substances, and advised his three sons to give their wives over to the princes of the three other elements.

Cordeliers of Orleans

The Cordeliers of Orleans were ordered to make full apology and were publicly exposed because they had sequestered a novice in their church and had forced her to play the role of a ghost. The court order was issued in 1534 and called for the banishment of Friars Colimant, Darras, Bressin, Brossier . . . and Legay.

Correspondence with the Devil

Among those who have carried on correspondence with

the devil is Berbiguier, author of *The Goblins,* published in Paris in 1821. The first letter at the end of his collection is addressed to him by the sorcerer Moreau and the witch Vandeval, and bears the seal of the infernal and invisible committee. . . . The second letter is signed by Lucifer and is written at the direction of Beelzebub.

Courtinière

A Breton gentleman named Courtinière found fault with his wife, and although he spoke to her kindly and candidly, she resolved to avenge herself. . . . She bribed two of the servants and persuaded them to strangle her husband. They carried his body down to a cellar in the castle, where they dug a trench and buried him. The next day the woman announced that her husband had gone away on a trip, and shortly thereafter she said that he had been killed in the woods. . . . The brother of the deceased was walking in the garden when his nose started to bleed. He was startled since nothing like this had ever happened to him before. At the same time it seemed to him that he saw the ghost of Courtinière, and that the ghost was beckoning him to follow. He followed the specter as far as the cellar, where he watched it disappear. . . . Eventually the corpse was discovered and identified. The guilty were arrested and sentenced.

Cross-roads

Places where four roads meet. Sorcerers meet ordinarily at cross-roads to celebrate the sabbat. In several provinces people still point out dreaded cross-roads in the middle of which were placed stakes that sorcerers or demons surrounded with lanterns during the nocturnal orgy. One can still observe on the ground a wide circle inside which the demons danced, and it is said that grass will not grow there.

Curses

Sicknesses or misfortunes brought about by some infernal art are said to be the result of curses that can be broken only by a supernatural power. Seven main types of curses or spells are employed by sorcerers: (1) They put a criminal love for the wife of another woman in the heart of a man; (2) inversely, they cause one person to hate or envy another; (3) they prevent bewitched husbands from engendering their own kind; (4) they cause sicknesses; (5) they bring about the death of people; (6) they deprive men of their reason; (7) they destroy the property of their enemies and reduce them to a state of poverty. . . . One can ward off evil spells by washing his hands with urine in the morning. . . . Sorcerers, when they remove a curse, are obliged to place it on something more important than the possessor; otherwise it will return. But a sorcerer cannot remove a curse if he is held captive. To remove a curse, he must have full freedom.

D

Danis

On Friday, May 1, 1705, at five o'clock in the afternoon, Danis Milanges, the son of a lawyer, fell victim, at the age of eighteen to such singular afflictions . . . that the doctors were baffled. He reported that he had seen a shepherd whom he did not know, and that the shepherd had said to him: "Sir, turn back; your horse will not advance." The young man laughed at the shepherd's words, but he was unable to make his horse go forward and was obliged to lead him back home, where he fell sick because the shepherd had put a curse on him. . . . Father Lebrun, who reports this extraordinary happening at length, is convinced that witchcraft was the cause, but the poor boy's delusions were actually produced by epilepsy.

Death

Poetic because it has to do with things immortal, mysterious because of its silence, death was supposed to have countless ways of announcing its arrival. Sometimes the first hint of approaching death was the ringing of a bell of its own accord; sometimes the man who was about to die heard three thuds on the floor of his room. . . . The Chinese believe that the dead return to their home once every year on the last night of the year. Throughout the night, they leave the door open in order that their deceased relatives may come in as soon as they arrive. . . . The Japanese are very sad when sickness comes upon one of their relatives, but they evidence the greatest joy at the moment of their death. They imagine that sicknesses are invisible demons. . . . The Turks, when they bury the dead, leave their legs free in order that they may kneel when the angels come to examine them, for they believe that the soul returns to the body as soon as it is placed in the grave. . . . Others say that those who are dying see demons, and that the Virgin asked to be exempt from their visitation. In Brazil the dead are guarded for several nights to prevent demons from carrying them to hell. . . . The Armenians rub their dead with oil, for they think that they must struggle physically with evil spirits.

Demoniacs

A demoniac is one possessed by an evil spirit. The people whom the devil has chosen to use as his abode suffer varying degrees of torment, depending on the phase of the moon. The historian Joseph says that it is not a demon but the soul of a wicked person that penetrates the body of the one possessed and torments him. The Jews used roots and incantations to expel the devil. . . . There were several ways of determining that a person was a demoniac . . . including facial swelling, grimaces, insensitivity and leprosy, immobility, twitchings of the stomach, staring, French answers to Latin questions, and the absence of bleeding from cuts.

Desbordes

Valet to the duke of Lorraine, Charles IV. He was accused, in 1628, of hastening the death of Princess Christine, the mother of the duke, and of having caused several maladies which the doctors attributed to his evil spells. . . . On one occasion he took it upon himself to resuscitate four men who had been hanged (for he always did everything by threes). Frightened by his unnatural acts, Charles IV tried to procure evidence against him. He was given his day in court, sentenced to be burned, and executed.

Deshoulières

Madame Deshoulières decided to spend a few months on an estate four leagues from Paris and was invited to choose the most beautiful room in the castle, with the exception of one room that was visited nightly by a ghost. For a long time Madame Deshoulières had wanted to see a ghost, and in spite of all the objections raised, she moved into the very room that was haunted. When night came she went to bed, took a book, as was her custom, read and then, having finished, turned out the light and fell asleep. She was soon awakened by a noise at the door, which was hard to close. Someone opened it, came in, and walked heavily. . . . Stretching forth her hands, she seized two hairy ears, which she had the patience to hold until the next morning . . . when it was discovered that the presumed ghost was a big dog which found her room more comfortable for sleeping than the poultry-yard.

Deumus or Deumo

Divinity of the inhabitants of Calicut in Malabar. He is really only a devil worshiped under the name of Deumus. He has a crown, four horns on his head, and four crooked teeth in his mouth, which is enormous. He has a sharp, crooked nose, feet like those of a rooster, and holds in his claws a soul that he seems to be about to devour.

Devil

Name given to demons in general. It comes from a Greek word that designates Satan, "one fallen from heaven." In all countries the devil is popularly represented as a black monster; Negroes depict him as being white. In Japan the Shintoists are convinced that the devil is none other than the fox. They exorcise this animal as an evil spirit. In Africa the devil is generally respected. The Negroes along the Gold Coast never forget, before taking a meal, to throw a piece of bread on the ground for the evil spirit. . . . The inhabitants of the Philippines boast of conversing with the devil. They relate that some of them tried to speak alone with him and were killed by the wicked spirit; that is why they gather in great crowds when they wish to converse with the devil.

Devil's Barn

Popular tale. A farmer in Champagne, named Jean Mullin, lived happily and in peace from the produce of his farm, which he cultivated with his wife and children. But . . . thunder and lightning came, caused a fire, and reduced to ashes all the grain in his barn. One evening when he was walking along a road near a crossing . . . he saw a man coming toward him. The man inquired about his troubled expression, and the farmer related his hardships. The stranger told him that everything would be made right if the farmer would have faith in him. "I have supernatural powers," he said, "and your barn will be rebuilt before the cock crows if you consent to hand over to me the child now carried in her womb by your wife." The devil . . . finally persuaded him, and the unhappy father signed a pact with his blood, promising to hand over his child, as soon as it came to birth, to the bearer of the note. Catherine's pregnancy was about to come to an end. She suffered frightful pain and died in giving birth to a little girl . . . whom they named Antoinette. When she reached the age of fifteen, she was well developed and was becoming more and more beautiful. Her father decided to marry her off early in order to free himself from his dread over what the devil might do. One night . . . a specter sat down on her bed, took her hand, looked at her with his fiery eyes, and said: "You are mine forever! . . ." Afterwards, he disappeared. Later . . . Antoinette suffered frightful convulsions and the priest said that she was possessed, pronounced many conjurations . . . and forced the devil to come out, howling with rage.

Devil's Carriage

For many nights at the beginning of the seventeenth century, a black carriage drawn by black horses driven by a black coachman passed through a Parisian suburb . . . without making a sound. It seemed to depart every evening from the house of a man who had died a short time previously. The people were convinced that it must be the devil's carriage, with the man's body inside. Later the whole episode was discovered to be the work of a scoundrel intent upon gaining possession of the man's house. He had tied cushions to the wheels of the carriage and around the horses' hoofs to make his nightly escapade appear to be something supernatural.

Devil's Castle

Popular tale. Not far from the town of Utrecht people point with terror to the devil's castle. It is a strange, hideous structure built of stone and containing horrible paintings of demons with long tails, with bas-reliefs representing the damned, flames, and all the horrors of hell that can be imagined. For many years no one would live in this forbidding manor. The devil was said to have taken it as his residence. He was supposed to go there on the thirteenth of each month to celebrate the sabbat and to perform his orgies . . . and twenty persons were said to have had their necks broken as they sought to enter such a dangerous place with impunity.

Devil's Chain

The old women in Switzerland preserve the legend that St. Bernard keeps the devil chained inside one of the mountains that surround the abbey in Clairvaux. On this legend is based the custom of the Swiss marshals: every Monday before taking up their duties, they strike the anvil three times with a hammer, as if to tighten the devil's chain and prevent his escape.

Devil's Wall

A famous wall that once separated England and Scotland. Several parts, unchanged by the ravages of time, still remain. The strength of the cement and the hardness of the stones have convinced the residents of the region that it was built by the devil's hand. The most superstitious people take great pains to gather up even the tiniest fragments, which they put into the foundations of their houses in order to confer upon them the solidity of the wall. It was built by Hadrian.

Divining rod

A forked branch from a tree — hazel, alder, beech, or apple — used to discover metals, hidden streams, treasures, crimes and thieves. For a long time skilled men have used rods to perform marvels; and since Moses' rod, every magician has had his wand or rod. Their possession is attributed to fairies and to powerful sorcerers. Medea, Circe, Mercury, Bacchus, Zoroaster, Pythagoras, Pharo's sorcerers all had their rods, and Romulus used a divining rod when he uttered his prophecies. . . . The talent for making the divining rod turn is given to only a few privileged beings. One can easily determine whether one has received it naturally . . . by cutting a forked branch from a hazel-tree and holding one of the two tips in each hand. When his foot is placed on top of the object that is being sought, or on clues that may indicate the location of the object, the rod will turn independently in the searcher's hands and will be an infallible guide. Aymar was skilled in its use . . . and the bishop of Morienne was able to identify both true and spurious relics of saints. . . . No less astounding is the fact that the rod turns only when the holder intends for it to turn. Thus when a stream of water is to be identified, the rod will not turn when the diviner passes over hidden treasure or clues to a murder.

Dog

Dogs were ordinarily faithful companions of magicians. Actually it was the devil who took the form of a dog in order that he might follow magicians without arousing suspicion. He was always recognized, however, in spite of his disguise. . . . Black always betrays the presence of the devil under the dog's skin. The ancient magicians also believed that demons revealed themselves as dogs, and Plutarch in his life of Cimon relates that a demon, disguised as a black dog, came to Cimon to announce his approaching death. The same ridiculous belief caused Christians to drive dogs away from their churches. Among the ancients the furies were called the dogs of hell, and black dogs were sacrificed to the infernal deities. But some people had other ideas, and the dog has even been singled out for special honors. . . . In Ethiopia a dog was king, and his barking and nuzzling were interpreted as signs of his anger or of his pleasure.

Dragon

Dragons have stirred up much interest, but they are no longer seen. They were, it is said, winged serpents. Philostratus says that to become sorcerers and soothsayers the Arabs ate the heart or the liver of a flying dragon. . . . The devil often bears the name *ancient dragon* and has at times taken the shape of this legendary animal. . . .

St. Pol, bishop of Leon, had tamed a dragon, which was sixty feet long, and taught him to follow him like a little dog. It is said that the dragon mentioned by Posidonius covered an acre of land and swallowed a fully armed knight as if he were a pill. But that was only a tiny dragon in comparison with the one discovered in India. According to Maximus of Tyre, it covered five acres of land.

Dung

Since man is the noblest of all creatures, his excrement has a peculiar, extraordinary property with respect to the treatment of several diseases. Dioscorides and Galen stress the point and insist that it cures diseases of the throat and quinsies. . . . When applied to the sting of a bee or a hornet, it immediately soothes the pain. Here is a secret . . . beauty preparation: Take the dung of small lizards, tartar of white wine, scrapings from a hartshorn, white coral and rice flour in equal proportions; crush and mix in a mortar; wet the fine mixture in distilled water and add an equal amount of almonds, slugs, and white mullein petals; then blend in an equal quantity of white honey and stir the whole concoction. It should be stored in a silver or glass container, and should be applied to the face, hands and throat.

E

Elisabeth of Hoven

Nun in the convent of Hoven during the twelfth century. One day she saw the devil in her bedroom. Since she recognized him by his horns, she went up to him and gave him a slap that sent him flying. . . . On another occasion she thought at first that a man had made his way into the convent, but when she was convinced that she was dealing with the devil, Sister Elisabeth exclaimed: "Oh! If I had known that, what a blow I would have given him!"

Eurynome

Demon belonging to a higher order, prince of death, according to some demonologists. He has enormous, long teeth, a hideous body covered with sores, and a fox-skin clothing. He was known to the pagans. Pausanias says that he feeds on the corpses of the dead. There was in the temple at Delphi a statue showing him with a dark skin and the huge teeth of a famished wolf; he was sitting on the skin of a vulture.

Exorcisms

Formulas used by saints, magicians and priests to evoke or expel spirits. , . . . To exorcise a spirit, one must first fast for three days, have masses sung, and say several prayers. . . . Then one must find and light a candle blessed on Candlemas Day, secure a cross, holy water, and an incenser; recite the seven psalms of penitence and the Gospel of St. John while approaching the abode of the spirit; kneel and recite humbly the following prayer: "Lord Jesus Christ . . . we humbly implore your gracious pardon . . . in the name of the Father, and of the Son, and of the Holy Ghost. Amen." The formula for exorcising the four principal devils is attributed to St. Cyprian, Bishop of Carthage. Many rituals and lengthy prayers are required, along with fumigations and sulphur, which demons cannot smell. Prayers are a part of the ritual.

Eyes

Boguet states that witches have two eyeballs in one eye. Illyrian witches had the same peculiarity in both eyes. They mortally enchanted those at whom they looked, and they killed people at whom they gazed for a long time. . . . In many parts of Spain people are terrified by enchanters who use their eyes to poison their enemies. One Spaniard had such an evil eye that he caused the windows in a house to break by staring at them. . . . In Brittany, if the left eye of a dead person does not close, one of his nearest relatives is threatened by death.

F

Fatal Hour

"The Fatal Hour" is a popular tale of three young German girls. Having met one day, two of them asked the third, Florentine, why she was so sad. She told them the reason in these words: "My sister Seraphine . . . was obsessed with astrology. Once when she became sick, I noticed that she embraced my father and me with great affection . . . 'The clock will soon strike nine,' she said. 'Think of me.' . . . She clasped our hands and, when the clock struck nine, fell back on her bed, never to rise again. Later . . . my father said in a faint voice: 'When the clock strikes nine, my fatal hour, according to Seraphine's prediction, will have come . . . do not fail to read the paper that I am giving to you.' The sound of the clock as it struck nine, the fatal hour for my father, drove me . . . insane. Count Ernest," she continued, "had asked for my hand in marriage . . . and I had consented. I therefore lost no time in . . . reading my father's letter. 'Seraphine has probably told you already,' it said, 'that when she tried to question the specter about your fate, it immediately disappeared. The invisible being that she saw told her that three days before the day set for your marriage, you would die at the fatal hour.'" Florentine stopped and said: "Now you see, dear friends, the cause of my sadness . . . tomorrow the count is to return from his voyage. The ardor of his love caused him to set the date for our marriage three days after his return, which is today!" The clock struck the fatal hour. Seraphine appeared before her sister. Florentine clasped her in her arms and died, saying: "Forever yours."

Flaque (Louis-Eugéné)

A well known sorcerer who was brought to trial at Amiens in 1825. He was accused of using magic tricks and cabbalistic practices to swindle people. . . . In March, 1825, the royal court of Amiens convicted him and two of his accomplices of using fraud to convince certain others of the existence of a supernatural poser . . . and of persuading them to hand over the sum of four hundred and ninety-two francs.

Flauros

Grand general of hell. He appears in the shape of a terrible leopard. When he assumes a human shape, he has a frightful face and blood-red eyes. He knows the past, the present and the future. He incites demons or spirits against his enemies the exorcists, and he commands twenty legions.

Forcas, Forras or Furcas

Knight and grand president of hell. He appears in the shape of a strong man with a long beard and white hair. He is mounted on a big horse and holds a sharp spear in his hand. He knows the properties of herbs and precious stones, and he teaches logic, esthetics, chiromancy, pyromancy and rhetoric. He can make a man invisible, inventive, and adept in the use of words. He can locate lost objects and discover hidden treasure. He has at his command twenty-nine legions of demons.

Fright

A schoolboy in whom teachers had instilled morbid fear of the devil and evil spirits had let his imagination run wild, with the result that at the age of fifteen he was unable to lie down alone in a room without dying of fright for two hours before falling asleep. . . . Piron often related that when he was about ten years old, frightful cries were heard one winter evening. They seemed to be coming from the house of a cooper who lived nearby. Piron and his family went to investigate. . . . "Oh! Have mercy!" said the cooper, trembling. "On returning this evening . . . I had to be rather rude to my wife, who thought I was drunk. She threatened me and left. I undressed and was about to lie down when I was struck on the rear by a red-hot iron bar. . . . None other than Lucifer could have struck such a blow." He was allowed to endure the full force of fright for a while, and this had a favorable effect on his drunkenness.

Frogs

It is commonly believed in England that frogs pass water. . . . As for their croaking, St. Grengoul was so upset by it, while he was saying mass, that he tied their tongues and made them mute. The lamas in Tartary explain earthquakes in this way: When God formed the earth, he placed it on the back of a big frog; and every time the animal shakes his head or stretches out his legs, he makes the part of the earth above him tremble. . . . The brush frog, when chopped up and rubbed over the kidneys, makes dropsical persons urinate so much that they are cured.

G

Gabrielle d'Strées

Mistress of Henry IV, died in 1599. She is known to have tried to marry the king. She was pregnant for the fourth time and was living in the home of Zamet, famous financier. . . . While walking in the garden, she suffered a severe heart attack. She had a bad night, and on the following day experienced such frightful convulsions that she turned completely black and her mouth twisted until it was at the back of her neck. She expired under great torment, and horribly disfigured. . . . Several people charged the devil with this charitable act. It was said that he had strangled her to prevent a scandal and to avoid further disturbances.

Galactite or Milkstone

Blackish stone to which some writers attribute several miraculous properties, among them the property of protecting the bearer against flies and other insects. To put it to the test, a man was rubbed with honey during the summertime and told to carry the stone in his right hand. If he passed the test, the stone was said to be genuine. It was also believed to have the power to disclose the secrets of others when carried in the mouth.

Games of Chance

One can always win in a game of chance by wearing a cross and these words written on virgin parchment: *Aba aluy* + *abafroy* + *agera* + *procha*. One can charm dice or cards so as to win constantly by blessing them with three signs of the cross and repeating these words: *Partiti sunt vestimenta mea, miserunt sortem contra me ad incarte cla a filii a Eniol Liebee Braya Braguesca et Belzebuth.*

Garters

Magic garters for travelers are fashioned as follows. First gather the herb known as wormwood or artemisia. This should be done just as the sun is entering into the first sign of Capricorn. Allow the wormwood to dry in the shade and use the skin of a young hare to fashion it into a garter. . . . When worn on your legs, it will prevent any man on horseback from following you for a very long period of time. It was once believed that magicians could provide magic garters to enable a man to cover a great distance in a short time. That probably accounts for the origin of the notion of seven-league boots.

Gaufridi (Louis Jean-Baptiste)

Priest in Marseille who was reputed to be a sorcerer. He lived near the end of the sixteenth century. The devil is said to have appeared to him one day while he was reading a book on magic. They struck up a conversation and became acquainted with each other. The priest, seemingly charmed by his horned majesty's good qualities, made a formal pact in which he surrendered his soul to the devil in exchange for the power to seduce all the women and girls of his choosing by simply blowing on their faces (instead of having to flatter them). He fell in love with the daughter of a nobleman, Madeleine de la Palud. . . . The girl, apparently frightened, or fickle, or dissatisfied, suddenly left him and sought seclusion in a

Ursuline convent. Furious, Gaufridi sent a legion of devils after her. All the nuns thought they were possessed, and the witchcraft of the poor priest was authenticated. A decree of the parliament of Provence condemned him to be burned, in April, 1611.

Generation

It is very important, as Avicenna states, to know what is going on at the time a child is begotten. Thus it is advisable to examine carefully the arrangement of the heavens and to choose as the moment for procreation the hour when the good planets are dominant. Albert the Great had a secret for engendering at will a boy or a girl. Husband and wife should pulverize the womb and the entrails of a hare and drink the powder dissolved in wine. The woman will give birth to the boy. . . . It they pulverize the liver and testicles of shoat and drink the powder dissolved in pale white wine, the woman will give birth to a girl.

Ghosts

Spirits or specters that bode ill and that terrified our

predecessors even though they knew that there was no reason to fear them when armed with nettle and milfoil. The Jews believe that a ghost cannot recognize the person that he is attempting to frighten if that person's face is covered by a veil. When a person is guilty, however, Buxtorf adds, God rips away the mask so that the spirit can see and bite the culprit. . . . Ghosts have often been known to give advance warning of death. A specter appeared for that purpose at the wedding of the king of Scotland, Alexander III, who died shortly thereafter. Countless other examples could be given.

Ghouls

It seems that the belief in vampires, ghouls and lamia, which are all related types of specters, has been prevalent since time immemorial among the Arabs, Persians, Greeks and all nations of the East. . . . In Caylus' *Oriental Tales* we find a kind of vampire that can prolong his odious existence only by eating from time to time the heart of a young man. A host of similar characteristics appear in stories translated from Arabic. These stories prove that horrible notions of vampirism have deep roots in Arabia.

Girard (Jean-Baptiste)

Jesuit, born around 1680 in Dôle. . . . He became famous, much to his sorrow, because of the most scandalous accusations. He was proved to have bewitched and seduced Cadière, and that he was guilty of the crimes of witchcraft, quietism, spiritual incest, abortion . . . and subornation of witnesses.

Goblins

Household imps or spirits that hide in remote places and under piles of wood. They must be given the most tasty foods, for they will steal for their masters wheat found in neighboring barns. The Gobelin works in Paris are said to be named for goblins who originally came there to work and who taught other workers to make beautiful tapestries.

Godeslas

When the first crusade was preached in the diocese of Maestricht, a papal bull allowed the old, the poor and the infirm to be exempt from the trip to the Holy Land on payment of a certain sum of money. . . . A miller named Godeslas, who was rich, old and a usurer, made arrangements to pay only five marks for the privilege to stay behind with his asses and operate his mill. But merciful Heaven wanted to show him . . . what he was missing, and turned him over to Satan . . . who took him down to Hell. Among the others, Godeslas recognized his father, his mother and his other relatives. He was shown a flaming chair and told: "You will die in three days . . . and return here to spend eternity on this burning chair." Then the devil took him back to his mill. Because he talked of hell, the devil, death and a burning chair . . . they sent for a priest. "I have no need of confession," he said. "My fate is sealed. . . ." He died without contrition, without confession, without a viaticum. And he went straight to hell.

Grace

St. Gregory the Great reports that the devil turned himself into a head of lettuce one day, and that a young nun ate him in her salad. The consequences were serious. The nun had not said grace before the meal and found herself possessed by the demon. Fortunately Equitius, a holy man, was able to exorcise the demon. . . . A young nun was tormented so vehemently by the devil that she won the sympathy of all the sisters. The unclean spirit jumped provocatively on her bed, grasped her in his arms, and violated her in every way. The experts were consulted, but to no avail; and prayers, confessions, signs of the cross had no effect on the stubborn demon. The nun finally turned to a pious person who gave her this advice: "When the devil tries to approach, pray and you will certainly be left alone." The sister followed his instructions, and the devil actually was forced to withdraw. It is even said that he never returned.

Grandier (Urbain)

The Ursuline convent established in London in 1626 soon became haunted by ghosts and evil spirits. Several nuns stated that they had been possessed . . . and their director, Jean Mignon, resolved to turn the event to the glory of God and at the same time to discredit Urbain Grandier, the vicar of St. Peter's in London. Grandier was accused of having used magic to bewitch the nuns. The bishop of Poitiers condemned him without hearing his defense. He was taken to the stake . . . where he continued to proclaim his innocence until they threw holy water in his face. As the flames began to make his tormentors uncomfortable, they withdrew. A flock of pigeons wheeled around the stake. Those who believed in possession shouted that these were demons who had come to try to save Grandier; others said that the innocent pigeons had appeared, in the absence of men, to bear witness to his innocence. Finally a huge fly buzzed around his head. A monk, who had read in a decree that devils always appear to tempt men at the hour of their death, and who had heard that Beelzebub meant in Hebrew "Lord of the Flies," suddenly shouted that the fly buzzing around his head was Beelzebub, who had come to take the vicar's soul to hell.

H

Hand of the Hanged Man

The hand of a man who has been hanged should be wrapped in a strip from a mortuary shroud. It should be wrapped tightly enough to squeeze out any remaining blood, then put into an earthen container, together with salt, saltpeter . . . and pepper. It should be left in the container for fifteen days, then exposed to bright sun during dog days, until completely dried. Then a sort of candle should be prepared, using grease from the hanged man, virgin wax, and sesame from Lapland. The hand of the hanged man is used as a chandelier to hold the lighted candle. Wherever one goes with this fatal instrument, those present will remain motionless, just as if they were dead.

Harppe

A Norman named Harppe was at the point of death. He ordered his wife to bury him in a standing position in front of the kitchen door in order that he might not be completely cut off from the smell of her stews . . . and might see what was going on in the house. The wife docilely and faithfully executed his command. But a few weeks after his death, he began to appear frequently in the form of a hideous ghost who killed workmen and molested the neighbors to such a degree that no one dared remain in the village. One peasant, named Olaus Pa, was bold enough to attack the vampire. He struck him a hard blow with a lance and left the weapon in the wound. The specter disappeared, and Olaus had the dead man's tomb opened the next day . . . and found his lance in Harppe's body.

Hélias (Jean)

A gentleman wrote that he had gone, on Sunday, New Year's Day in 1623, to Notre-Dame in Paris to talk about the conversion of his lackey, Jean Hélias. "I finally found him half-asleep by the fire," the gentleman wrote. "His head was propped against the wall and his eyes and mouth were open. I said to him: 'Get up, you sot!' 'Sire,' he answered, 'I am lost, I am dead, the devil has just tried to make off with me.' He reported that he had heard a voice which he had at first assumed to be mine, but that on discovering the truth, he had made the sign of the cross, saying: 'In the name of the Father, the Son and the Holy Ghost, and may the Virgin Mary help me.' The persistent devil disappeared. He came back several times, but had no success. Hélias was converted, and everything turned out well."

Hell

The ancients, most of our contemporaries, and cabbalists especially locate hell in the center of the earth. Dr. Swinden in his research on fire and hell assumes that hell is in the sun "because the sun is everlasting fire." Others have added that the damned are forever engaged in keeping the fire burning, and that the spots that appear on the round surface of the sun following great catastrophes are produced simply by the excessive number of people sent there. . . . We read in the Bible that no mortal has returned from hell, but we have testimony from several pious chroniclers that several other trustworthy people have made the journey in flesh and .bone and have returned with their reports on events in hell. Among these is the account of an English monk whose activities are related in the first person: "I had St. Nick as my guide. He led me down a flat road to a huge, horrible place teeming with dead people that were being tormented in a thousand terrifying ways."

Henry III

Son of Catherine de Medici rumored to be a sodomite and a sorcerer. Seditious pamphlets were written about him. One of these accused him of conducting lessons in magic at the Louvre. . . . He was also accused of procuring a prostitute for his favorite devil. . . . Here is an extract from a seditious pamphlet entitled *Witchcraft of Henry of Valois,* which appeared a few months before his assassination: "He . . . made public profession of his witchcraft. In his house was found a trunk filled with writings on witchcraft. . . . Recently in the forest at Vincennes two silver satyrs were discovered, along with the skin of a child."

Heraides

Daughter of Diophantus, born in Macedonia. When she had reached nubility, her father gave her in marriage to a man named Samiades. After he had been married one year, Samiades went on a long voyage. During his absence his wife Heraides came down with a strange sickness: her sexual organs became like a phlegmon. . . . On the seventh day the rupture of the phlegmon suddenly occurred, and out came a male organ. Heraides . . . returned to her father's house and continued to dress as a woman. . . . Samiades returned from his voyage and went to the father's house. The father . . . wanted Heraides to divorce him, but the court ordered her to return to her husband.

Rising, she disrobed in the presence of the judges, showed them that she was a man, and asked them if the law required a man to serve as a wife to another man. . . . She renamed herself Diophantus, and followed Alexander, the king of Syria, to war.

I

Imagination

Dreams, reveries, chimeras, instances of panic, superstitions, prejudices, marvelous or extraordinary occurrences, castles in Spain, happiness, fame, and stories of spirits and ghosts, sorcerers and devils, are all products of the imagination. . . . Torquemada relates that a husband was going to a masked ball disguised as a devil. He decided to make love to his wife while dressed in this manner. She gave birth to a monster with the face of a demon. . . . But such phenomena are generally exaggerations. Monstrous fetuses are variously looked upon as having the shape of a dog, a pig, a hare, etc. . . . even though they have no definite shape. A man as ugly as Aesop was able to have handsome children because he constantly set beautiful paintings before his wife.

Incubuses

Lewd, lecherous demons that bother women and girls. Servius Tullius, a Roman king, was the offspring of a beautiful slave and Vulvan, according to some authors; according to other of the cabbalists, however, he was fathered by a salamander; and according to demonographers, he was the offspring of an incubus. . . . A Scottish girl was impregnated by the devil. Her parents asked her who had made her pregnant, and she replied that the devil slept with her every night, in the shape of a handsome youth. The parents slipped into her room by night . . . and saw beside her a horrible monster. The priest was called in to expel the monster, but as he escaped, he made a frightful noise, burned the furniture in the room, and carried away the roof of the house. Three days later the girl gave birth to a monster, the vilest one imaginable, and the midwives strangled it to death.

L

Leaupartie

Norman nobleman . . . who wanted to have Heurtin as his priest, and who published in 1735 a memoir to establish the fact that his children and other girls who had imitated their extraordinary behavior were possessed. He turned to the bishop of Bayeux for exorcists. Heurtin sent an inquiry to the faculty of medicine at the Sorbonne to find out whether the phenomenon could be explained by natural causes. He noted that the demoniacs understood Latin, that they were malicious, that they spoke like heretics, libertines and atheists, that they did not like the sounds of bells, that they barked like dogs. . . . The rites of exorcism were conducted publicly by Heurtin and the priest from Neuilly. . . . But the demon was so tenacious that Charpentier, the well-known exorcist from Paris, came himself to perform the exorcism. To celebrate the presence of the holy man, the demoniacs created an uproar in the chapel. . . . The daughters of Leaupartie were separated and placed in communities surrounding the town of Caen. They were later returned in a more tranquil state of mind.

Leshies

A sylvan spirit or wood demon in Russian folklore. The Russians depict leshies as having a human body from the head to the waist, and the ears and beard of a goat; and, from the waist down, the body of a he-goat. When they walk in the fields, they shrink to the height of the grass, but when they run through the forests, they are as tall as the highest trees. Their screams are terrifying. They . . . mislead strollers by imitating the voice of an acquaintance, take them to their caves, and tickle them until they die.

Luxembourg (Francois de Montmorency)

Marshal of France, born in 1628 and died in 1695. He was accused of having made a pact with the devil. One of his men, Bonard, turned to Father Lesage for help in locating some misplaced papers. The priest ordered him to visit churches, recite psalms, and confess. He did all that was required of him, but the missing papers were not located. They were in the hands of a girl named Dupin. Bonard . . . performed a conjuration in the name of the marshal and laid a curse on Dupin to force her to turn over the papers. She refused . . . and Bonard had the marshal sign a pact with the devil. The pact was introduced as evidence at his trial. Lesage testified that the marshal had enlisted his and the devil's help in killing Dupin. . . . The trial lasted fourteen months. No verdict was rendered either for or against the marshal. He returned to the court and resumed his duties as captain of the guard. Louis XIV promulgated an ordinance in July, 1682, against those reputed to be soothsayers, magicians and enchanters.

M

Maillat (Louise)

Young demoniac who lived in 1598. She lost the use of her limbs and was taken to the Church of the Holy Redeemer for exorcism. She was found to be possessed by five demons called wolf, cat, dog, doll, and griffon. Two of the demons came out through her nose in the shape of fist-sized balls, one as red as fire and the other, the cat, completely black. The other demons left her less violently. Once they were outside her, all the demons circled the fire several times and disappeared. It was discovered that Françoise Secretain had made the little girl swallow the devils in a dung-colored crust of bread.

Magic

Magic provides those who possess it with an irresistible power. With the tap of a wand, a word, a sign, they control the elements, change the immutable order of nature, deliver the world to the infernal powers, unleash tempests, winds and thunder. . . . Magicians and witches are borne through the air . . . and can walk on water. Since they have faithful servants among their infernal cohorts, magicians have little difficulty in appropriating for themselves, without arousing suspicion, the goods of others. Examples include magicians who had their neighbors' grain brought to their barns and female magicians who, according to Delrio, had the devil milk their neighbors' cows and bring the milk to them.

Magic Circles

It is almost impossible to summon up demons unless one stands inside a circle. This keeps them from doing harm, for their first movement would be destructive in the absence of some semblance of order. The *Great Book of Spells* states that when entering the circle one must have in his possession no base metals but only gold or silver. . . . The coin must be concealed inside a folded white paper on which nothing has been written and sent to the spirit to prevent him from doing harm. While the spirit is bending over to pick up the coin . . . one pronounces the conjuration. The circles which sorcerers make for their dances at the sabbat are also called fairy circles, for fairies were believed to outline such circles when they danced in the moonlight.

Magic Girdles

Several occult books teach that all sorts of diseases can be cured by wearing a girdle made of ferns gathered on St. John's Eve, at midnight, and arranged in such a way as to form the magic character HVTY. . . . There are other magic girdles; for example, St. Margaret's girdle, which is supposed to facilitate childbirth. The same property is attributed to St. Oyan's girdle. Boguet cites a certain Perrette Girod . . . who attributed her ability to bear a child to St. Oyan's girdle and who, though formerly a heretic, afterward embraced Catholicism.

Magicians

Art of producing in nature things beyond the power of men, with help of demons and through certain ceremonies. There are two kinds of magic: natural magic . . . and ceremonial magic, which consists in the invocation of demons following the making of a formal or tacit pact with the infernal powers. The different branches of magic are cabala, enchantment, witchcraft, evocation of the dead or maleficent spirits, the discovery of hidden treasures and dark secrets, divination, the gift of prophecy, healing through magic formulas . . . and participation in the celebration of the sabbat. Natural magic is the art of predicting the future and producing extraordinary effects through natural means. . . . Black or diabolical magic, taught by the devil and practiced under his influence, is the art of invoking demons . . . and performing supernatural things.

Mallebranche

Remarkable story of the woman's ghost that appeared . . . five years after the woman had died. On Tuesday, December 11, 1618, a man named Mallebranche heard a noise outside his house on the Rue Sainte-Geneviève in Paris. Since he was not expecting anyone to call, he asked who was there. A faint voice answered that it was his wife . . . "Don't you recognize my voice?" she continued. "I am your wife, and I warned you that you would have to do penance or die." Later . . . he heard another voice saying: "Your wife is in great pain, but if you go to St. Cloud and pray for her, and burn five candles for the salvation of her soul, you will ease her pain." He went to St. Cloud and did as he had been instructed to do.

Malphas

Grand president of hell, who appears in the shape of a crow. When he appears as a human being, his voice sounds hoarse. He builds impregnable fortresses and towers, tears down the ramparts of his enemies, provides good workmen, makes available familiar spirits, receives sacrifices, double-crosses those who offer him sacrifices. He commands forty legions.

Mandragora

Good-natured familiar demons. They appear in the shape of beardless little men with thin hair. . . . The name is also applied to little puppets inhabited by the devil and consulted by sorcerers in time of crisis. The ancient Germans also had mandragoras that they called Alrunes. These were wooden figures that they worshiped, just as the Romans worshiped their lares. The Alrunes were supposed to protect houses and the people who lived in them. . . . Anyone fortunate enough to have the little figures thought that he had nothing to fear and expected only the best, particularly good health and the curing of diseases that resisted all types of treatment. Even more remarkable, they were thought to predict the future, either by a nod of the head or by speaking out intelligibly to their happy owners. . . . The ancients attributed miraculous powers to the plant called mandrake. It was supposed to increase fertility among women. The best roots were those that had been soaked in the urine of one who had been hanged.

Marguerite

An Italian woman who had a familiar spirit. According to Cardan, "There was in Milan a woman named Marguerite who told everyone that she had a devil or a familiar spirit that followed her everywhere. . . . She would invoke the spirit in her own language, and it would suddenly appear and answer her. The spirit's voice was not heard beside her but from afar, as if coming from a hole in a wall. . . . The wretched woman is looked upon with such horror because of her spirit that no one will give her lodging or have anything to do with her."

Marlagrane (Marie)

Witch who said that she had often seen the devil copulate with vast numbers of women, and that his practice was to approach beautiful women from the front and ugly ones from the rear. Delancre notes that the devil prefers sodomy to the highest forms of normal pleasures. . . .

Mastication

The ancients thought that the dead ate in their graves. The idea . . . probably goes back to the custom of celebrating funeral feasts at the tomb of the deceased. Philippe Rherius and Michel Raufft . . . published treatises on the subject. They cite several instances where the dead have devoured their own flesh.

Mean Monk

Parisians tell many tales about a legendary ghost whom they call the Mean Monk. He roams the streets by night, twists the necks of those who show their heads at windows, and practices legerdemain. He seems to be some sort of imp. Maids and nurses used to frighten children by threatening them with the Mean Monk. The Bogy-man has now replaced him.

Melchom

Demon who carries the purse. He is the paymaster for all the public employees in hell.

Michel de Sahourspe

Sorcerer from Saxony who confessed to having seen a big devil and a little one at the sabbat; that the big devil used the little one as his aide-de-camp; that he had also kissed the big devil on his bottom and had been kissed on the same spot by the little one; and finally that the rump of the Grand Master of the Sabbat was a face, with the result that sorcerers were not kissing his rear but his rear face. Delancre adds that he acted as he did to mock God and his noblest creatures.

Miracles

Charlatans and fanatics, observing the gullibility of people in accepting as true all sorts of miracles, took advantage of their weakness . . . and arrogated to themselves powers which they could never have possessed in any other way. The Jesuits relate that when Father Anchieta, a missionary in Brazil, was too warm, he ordered the chickens to leap into the air and use their wings to provide a parasol for him. . . . The Orientals attribute the formation of a kind of stone that resembles a petrified melon to a miracle. The story is as follows: When Elijah was dwelling on Mt. Carmel, he saw a plowman carrying melons pass by his cave one day, and he asked him for one of the melons. But the plowman told him that he was carrying stones, not melons. To punish him, Elijah changed his melons into stones.

Money

Money that comes from the devil is generally counterfeit. Delrio relates that a man who had received from the devil a purse filled with gold, found in it the following day nothing but embers and smoke. An unknown man, passing through a village, met a fifteen-year-old youth who had an interesting face and a modest appearance. The stranger asked the youth if he wanted to be rich, and when the latter assented, gave him a folded paper and told him that he could make it produce as many coins as he wished so long as he did not unfold it; and that if he overcame his curiosity, he would soon become acquainted with his benefactor. The youth went home, took out his mysterious treasure, and watched as gold pieces spilled out. . . . But he was unable to resist the temptation to open it, and inside it he found cats' claws, bears' nails, toads' feet, and other things so horrible that he threw the paper in the fire, where it lay for an hour without being consumed. The gold pieces that he had taken from it disappeared, and he realized that he had been consorting with the devil.

Monks

A monk, provoked by excessively long abstinence, decided one day to cook an egg in his cell, using the heat from his lamp. The abbot, making his rounds, saw the light and observed through the keyhole that the monk was cooking a meal. He entered suddenly and reprimanded him sharply. The monk excused himself, saying that the devil had tempted him and suggested this ruse. Suddenly the devil himself appeared. He had been hiding under the table all the while. He shouted at the monk: "You lied in your beard. I had no part in this ruse. I have just learned it from you."

Morals

The devil sometimes takes a hand in the matter of morals. . . . A man who had no reason to find fault with his wife, since she was beautiful, ignominiously cast a covetous eye on his neighbor. She, though she had every reason to praise her husband, who was handsome and considerate, was perverse enough to look with favor on the covetous overture. . . . The devil would not let their act of adultery go unpunished. He quickly . . . prepared a charm and bound together man and woman. After long but futile efforts to free themselves, they called for help. Those who heard their shouts . . . were shocked by what they saw. Many public prayers and rituals were required to break the spell.

Mozart

Mozart was obsessed by the thought of death. One day when he was lost in melancholic revery, he heard a carriage stop outside his house. A servant announced that a stranger wished to speak to him. "I am carrying out the orders of an important person who told me to find you," said the stranger. . . . "He has just lost a loved one and wishes to commemorate his death each year by having a solemn service performed, and he wants you to compose a *Requiem* for the service." Mozart was astounded by what he had heard . . . and promised to compose the *Requiem*. He set to work . . . and worked night and day . . . but his body was not equal to the strain. He fell unconscious one day. Later . . . he told his wife: "I am certain that I am writing the *Requiem* for my own funeral." The poor man . . . became obsessed with the notion that the stranger was not an ordinary being but that he had ties with the other world and had been sent to him to announce his approaching death. He worked harder and harder on the *Requiem* that he looked upon as his most lasting monument. . . . Finally the work was completed . . . and the stranger returned. Mozart was dead.

N

Ninon de l'Enclos

Alone in front of her mirror one day, when she was sixteen years old, Ninon de l'Enclos was admiring herself sadly. A voice suddenly answered her unspoken words, saying: "Isn't it terrible to be so pretty and to grow old?" She turned around quickly and saw with astonishment that a small black dwarf was standing beside her. . . . He continued: "If you will give yourself over to me, I will preserve your charms. At the age of forty-eight you will still be beautiful and will make conquests." Ninon reflected for an instant, then accepted his offer. The dwarf kept his word, and just before she died, she saw him standing at the foot of her bed, waiting for her.

Obereit (Jacques Hermann)

Alchemist and mystic, born in Arbon, Switzerland, in 1725, died in 1798. His father had also been fascinated by alchemy, which he called the art of perfecting metals through the grace of God. The son wished to profit by the instructions given him by his aged father. Since the family had been reduced to penury, Obereit worked without respite in his laboratory. . . . He married a person whom he called Theantis, the angelic shepherdess. "Our marriage," he said, "was neither Platonic nor Epicurean; it was midway between friendship and corporal union, a state probably unknown to the rest of the world." He published . . . a treatise on *The Relation of Spirits to Bodies Based on Newtonian Principles* (Augsburg, 1776).

P

Pact

There are several ways of making a pact with the devil. He can be summoned by reading the part about evocations in the *Great Book of Spells,* by reciting the formulas for conjuration given in this Dictionary, or by letting the blood from a chicken drip where two main roads cross and burying the chicken while reciting magic words. When the devil appears, one makes a pact with him and signs it with blood. The angel of darkness is not hard to deal with, provided of course that he receives the soul as a pledge.

Paul (Arnold)

Hungarian peasant crushed to death . . . under a load of hay in 1728. Thirty days after his death, four persons died suddenly as if attacked by vampires. People remembered that Arnold . . . had been tormented for a long time by a vampire . . . but had recovered after eating soil from the vampire's grave and rubbing himself with the vampire's blood. Paul's body was disinterred . . . his hair, his nails, and his beard had grown longer, his veins were filled with a liquid. A pointed stake was driven into his heart . . . and the vampire cried out piteously, as if he were alive.

Picard (Mathurin)

In charge of the convent of Louviers, he was accused of being a sorcerer and of having taken Madeleine Bavan to the sabbat. . . . Since he was dead at the time of her arrest, and since he was tried along with her and found guilty, his body was delivered to the executioner, dragged on a hurdle through streets and public places, and . . . burned. This happened in 1647.

Pierre de Brabancon

Charlatan born in Holland. Having fallen in love with a pretty Parisian girl . . . he soon learned to imitate her father's voice and managed . . . to obtain her hand in marriage. He stole her dowry, left Paris, and sought safety in Lyons, where a rich financier had just died, leaving a vast fortune to his son. Brabançon became acquainted with him and . . . induced him, again by imitating the voice of the young man's father, to give him six thousand francs.

Pipi

Witch who serves as cup-bearer at the sabbat. She pours drinks at mealtime not only for the king of hell but also for his officers and his disciples, who are sorcerers and magicians.

Plogojowits

Vampire that began to terrify the Hungarian village of Kisolova after he had been buried there for six weeks. During the past century he appeared by night in the homes of the sleeping inhabitants of the village . . . and caused the death of nine persons, both old and young, in the space of eight days. . . . These circumstances caused the villagers to decide to disinter his body. They found that it was still undecayed . . . that his hair and beard had grown out, and that his old nails had fallen out and been replaced by new ones. They also found fresh blood in his mouth — blood that the vampire had sucked from his victims. . . . They drove a sharp-pointed stake into his chest, and fresh red blood spurted out through his nose and mouth.

Popular Prognostications

When oaks bear many acorns, a long, harsh winter lies ahead. . . . Stars seen by day portend holocausts and wars. . . . Thunder in the evening will bring on a storm; thunder in the morning means wind; thunder at noon will be followed by rain. . . . Three suns are a sign of a triumvirate. Three suns were seen after the death of Julius Caesar and shortly before the reigns of Francis I, Charles V, and Henry VIII.

Possessed Persons

Gregory of Tours relates that in 531 Theodoric's army had entered the capital of Auvergne and soldiers had broken through the gates of the basilica of St. Julian. They pillaged the basilica and committed several acts of abomination, which caused them . . . to be possessed by the devil. Henry III had people who claimed to be possessed examined carefully. . . . Some Capuchins said that there was a demoniac in their midst. The king, skeptical, sent his surgeon Pigray and two other doctors to investigate. The woman who pretended to be possessed . . . was unable to answer satisfactorily questions put to her in Latin . . . and was placed in perpetual seclusion.

Poudot

Cobbler in Toulouse. The devil hid in his house in 1557. The evil spirit threw stones . . . and made such a stir that the chief magistrate came to see the extraordinary event. The devil knocked his hat off with a stone just as the magistrate was entering the room. . . . The magistrate fled, making the sign of the cross, and the spirit of darkness remained until driven out by exorcists.

Presentiments

Suetonius assures us that Calpurnia was tormented by dark presentiments a few hours before Caesar's death. But what is a presentiment? Is it an inner, secret voice? Is it a divine inspiration? Is it the presence of an invisible spirit that watches over our destinies? The ancients had made presentiment a sort of religion, and people today still believe in it.

Preservatives

Salgues notes that monks have always passed out, in exchange for a small sum of money, prayers, small bits of bread that has been blessed, and images and medallions to cure sicknesses. . . . Today in Brittany people still say that when a horse yawns, one must pronounce the words, "May St. Eloi help you!" because he is the patron saint of horses. Similarly, St. Hervé must be given butter to protect animals against wolves. The blind saint was guided by one of these animals.

Pruflas or Busas

Grand prince and grand duke of the infernal empire. He reigned in Babylonia, where he had the head of an owl. He stirs up strife, starts wars, initiates quarrels and reduces people to mendicity. He gives lengthy answers to all sorts of questions. He has at his command twenty-six legions.

R

Ralde (Marie de la)

Pretty witch arrested at the age of eighteen. She had begun to practice her craft at the age of ten and was taken to the sabbat for the first time by the witch Marissans. After the death of the latter, the devil himself took her to the assembly, where, according to Marie's statement, he assumed the shape of a tree . . . but sometimes appeared as an ordinary man now red, now black. She had never kissed the devil but had seen how it was done. . . . She added that she liked the sabbat so well that it was just like a wedding. The witches listened to music so sweet that it seemed as if they were in heaven . . . and the devil convinced them that the fire that burns forever was not real but artificial.

Rambouillet

The marquis of Rambouillet and the marquis of Précy, both between twenty-five and thirty years of age, were close friends. Before going away to war . . . they promised one another that the first one who died would come back to inform his companion. Months later . . . Précy heard a noise and saw Rambouillet, who told him that he had come to keep his promise; that everything said about the other world was absolutely right; that he ought to think seriously about changing his way of living; and that he had no time to lose, for he would be killed during his first engagement.

Red-Hot Test

A persons sentenced to undergo the red-hot test was forced to carry a red-hot iron bar weighing about three pounds for a distance of nine or twelve paces. The test might also involve putting the hand into an iron gauntlet just as the gauntlet was drawn from a furnace.

Ring

In times past there were many magic rings or rings bearing amulets. Workers of miracles healed by touching with their rings, and magicians made studded rings with which they performed marvels. The belief in magic rings was so widespread among the pagans that priests could not wear rings unless they were so unpretentious that it was evident that they contained no amulets. Magic rings were used extensively among the Christians, however, and many superstitions were attached to the *wedding-ring*. It was thought that the fourth finger, called the ring finger, was linked directly to the heart and that the wedding ring should be placed on no other finger. An old book of the occult states that the moment when the husband gives the ring to his bride in the presence of the priest is of the greatest importance. If the husband allows the ring to remain on the end of her finger and does not push it beyond the second joint, the woman will dominate him; but if he pushes the ring to the base of her finger, he will be her lord and master.

Robert

King of France. This pious monarch made the mistake of marrying his first cousin, with the consent of the bishops and with their dispensation. When Pope Gregory V was elevated to his pontificate, he convoked a council . . . and declared the king's marriage incestuous. King Robert, a good husband and a good father, refused to submit. He was excommunicated and his kingdom interdicted. One day when he was on his way to pray . . . a monk accosted him, showed him a monster with the neck and head of a drake, and said: "See . . . the terrible effects of your disobedience. Queen Bertha has gust given birth to this drake." The good king . . . repudiated his beloved Bertha, his excomunication was lifted, and his entourage returned.

Rodrigo

Last of the Gothic kings in Spain, famous for his crimes and debauchery during the first part of the eighth century. . . . He was in love with the daughter of Count Julian, one of the great lords of Spain. He seduced her, dishonored her, and banished her from the court. Count Julian . . . resolved to avenge himself . . . took his family to Africa, and promised all of Spain to the Moors in exchange for their help. The Spanish army . . . was torn to shreds, and Rodrigo vanished without a trace. Some said that he had been carried away by the devil.

Ronwe

Marquis and count of hell. He appears in the shape of a monster. He provides his adepts with knowledge of languages and with the goodwill of everyone. Nineteen infernal cohorts are under his orders.

S

Sabbat

An assembly of demons, sorcerers and witches, who gather to perform their nocturnal orgies. They generally devote their attention to planning or performing evil deeds, to instilling fear or fright in people, and to preparing spells and abominable mysteries. The sabbat is celebrated at a crossroad or in some wild, deserted place, near a lake or a pond, or near a marsh, where hailstorms and windstorms are created. The place where they assemble receives such a curse that neither grass nor anything else will grow there. . . . Witches often take to the sabbat, for different purposes, stolen children. If a witch promises to present to the devil the son or daughter of someone . . . and is unable to fulfill her promise, she must present her own child. Children who please the devil . . . are admitted into his kingdom, given a godfather and a godmother, forced to renounce God, the Virgin and the saints, and . . . marked in the left eye by one of Leonard's horns. Those . . . who show no promise are fried.

Sabbat Chalice

Pierre Delancre reports that when sorcerer priests say mass at the sabbat, they use a black host and a black chalice, and that at the moment of the elevation they pronounce these words: "Black crow! Black crow!"

Sabbat Dance

Pierre Pelancre maintains that sabbat dances make men lose their minds and cause women to have miscarriages. . . . The demons dance with the prettiest witches, either in the shape of a goat or of some other animal. They copulate in this manner with the witches, and so it is said that no woman or girl returns from these dances as chaste as she was before going there. . . . The dances are performed to the sound of a small drum, a flute, a violin, and another instrument that is struck with a stick. These are the only instruments employed, and yet sorcerers have stated positively that in this world no concert was ever better performed.

Shepherds

People are still convinced, in almost all our villages, that shepherds traffic with the devil, and that they are able very subtlely to practice mischief. It is very dangerous, they say, to go near shepherds without greeting them, for they lead offenders far astray, unleash storms ahead of them and open up precipices at their feet. Many terrible stories illustrate the point. . . . Although these poor people are illiterate, their lore and their power is feared to such an extent that in some villages travelers are warned not to insult them or to go near them without asking what time it is or how the weather will be, or something of the sort; otherwise, there may be heavy fog, or the travelers may be drowned by floods or risk great perils or lose their way along even the best routes.

Snails

Nowhere do we find that these good creatures have ever had any part in the sabbat. But it seems that there is something mysterious about them and that they might one day, when the studies that now engage our scholars are concluded, compete with the wireless telegraph. . . . Two friends separated by great distances will each be provided with a snail of the same species, and these will have been magnetized to insure their sympathy. Then the friend who has remained in Paris will deliver to his snail messages that he wishes to transmit to his friend in Peking, and the latter will reply in the same way.

Skepticism

A dubious, pusillanimous philosophy called Pyrrhonism, from the name of its author. Pyrrho lived about three hundred years before Christ. Diogenes Laertius assures us that he doubted everything . . . even going so far as to doubt the evidence provided by his own senses. This is not easy to believe, for Pyrrho may have reasoned like a fool, but he managed to live sensibly enough to reach the age of ninety.

Snow

St. Patrick is reported to have used snow to heat an oven. . . . One day when St. Francis was praying, the devil sought him out and tormented him with carnal temptations, St. Francis recognized his enemy, quickly disrobed, and whipped himself unmercifully. Afterwards he made seven small figures of snow and, taking them in his arms, shouted: "The biggest one is my wife, the next two are my sons, the fourth and fifth are my daughters, the sixth is my servant, and the seventh is my maid. Let's lose no time in warming them up or they will die of cold." At the same time he rolled over and over in the snow. . . . The devil went away, bewildered, and St. Francis went back to his cell.

Sorcerers

People who, with the help of infernal powers, can do whatever they please, as a consequence of their having made a pact with the devil. . . . While the French mercilessly burned every wretch accused of witchcraft, the English showed more wisdom and were satisfied simply to argue about witchcraft. . . . Sorcerers are guilty of fifteen major crimes, according to Bodin: (1) they deny God; (2) they practice blasphemy; (3) they worship the devil; (4) they consecrate their children to the devil; (5) they sacrifice their children to the devil before baptising them; (6) they consecrate their children to Satan while they are still in the womb; (7) they promise to bring everyone they can into the devil's service; (8) they are proud to swear by the devil's name; (9) they commit incest; (10) they kill, boil and devour people; (11) they feed on corpses and on men who have been hanged; (12) they use poison and witchcraft to kill people; (13) they destroy livestock; (14) they cause fruit to rot and bring on sterility; (15) they have carnal intercourse with the devil.

Sorcerers' Grease

The devil is supposed to use consecrated grease for his evil deeds. Witches rub themselves with the grease before going through the chimney to celebrate the sabbat. But in France witches believe that they can be transported astride a broom without the use of grease or unction. In Italy witches always keep a he-goat outside their house. . . . The inquisitors say that sorcerers receive their grease from the devil . . . who provides it for his own pleasure.

Spells (Casting of)

The casting of spells, whose invention is attributed by the rabbis to Shem, the son of Noah, was practiced by the ancients as well as by men today. This evil practice has always caused newlyweds to be afraid of sorcerers. The Greeks had a special law according to which any sorcerer or magician who through charms, incantations, ligatures, wax images or other evil practices charmed or enchanted anyone, or who used spells to bring about the death of men or beasts, were sentenced to die. . . . We find in Ovid and in Vergil the means through which spells were cast during their time. Sorcerers took a small wax figure which they wrapped in ribbons or in cords; they uttered incantations over its head as they drew the cords tight, one by one; then they stuck needles or nails into the region of the liver, completing the spell. . . . In cities today no one complains about sorcerers, but the casting of spells is still practiced in the villages of France. The practices described here are still popular, and . . . we live but a short distance from poor peasants who have their fortune-tellers, their sorcerers, their soothsayers, and who, fed on devilish superstitions, tremble at the thought of marriage.

Spirits

The ancients believed that spirits, which they called demons or jinni, were semi-gods. Each nation, says Apuleius, even each family and each man has a spirit to serve as his guide and to watch over his conduct. All nations had great respect for them, and the Romans revered them. They would not lay siege to towns or undertake wars until their priests had invoked their spirits. Caligula even decreed public punishment for those who cursed the spirits. . . . Cabbalists have held that spirits are material creatures, composed of the purest of all substances; that the power and activity of a spirit depends on the subtlety of its constituent matter. They identify two kinds of spirits, superior and inferior; the superior spirits are celestial or airy while the inferior spirits are aquatic or earthy. . . . According to the commonly held opinion, spirits are demons or devils that have remained in the air, in water, and on the earth. . . . Music may be used effectively against evil spirits, and we have proof of this through Saul, who managed to find peace of mind only through the sound of his harp.

Stolas

Grand prince of hell. He appears in the shape of an owl. When he assumes the shape of a man and appears before exorcists, he teaches astronomy, prophecy based on the study of plants, and the value of precious stones. Twenty-six legions look upon him as their general.

Succubuses

Demons who assume the shapes of women and seek out men. A very handsome young man was tormented every night by a female demon who came through his closed door and appeared at his bedside in the shape of a charming girl. He complained to his bishop, who made him fast, pray and go to confession. The beauty from hell ceased to torment him. St. Jerome tells of another Dulcinea from the dark empire . . . who tempted a bachelor. She had already raised goose pimples on him, and he was on the point of taking full advantage of his good fortune when she suddenly escaped from his arms. . . .

Swearing

It is shameful for Christians needlessly to repeat the name

of the devil. . . . A man just arising from bed says; "Where in the devil are my trousers?" Worse still . . . the expression is applied to good things. If a man does more than he is expected to do, we say that he works like the devil. . . . An angry father told his son to go to the devil. The devil went out and soon met the devil, who took him away. He was never seen again. Another man was irritated by the fact that his daughter drank a bowl of milk too hurriedly . . . and said he wished she could cram the devil into her stomach. Immediately the girl was aware of the presence of the devil, and she remained possessed until the day of her marriage. An ill-tempered husband told his wife to go to the devil, and immediately, as if he had come right out of the husband's mouth, the devil went through the poor woman's ear and into her body.

T

Tanchelin

In 1125 a heretic named Tanchelin was revered to such a degree in some provinces that people drank his urine and preserved his excrement as a relic. The money that came to him . . . enabled him to have good food and superb service. Fathers and husbands begged him to sleep with their daughters and wives.

Thou

One night in 1598 President Thou was awakened in the town of Saumur . . . by the weight of an enormous mass that was pressing down on his feet. The president shook off the weight and heard it strike the floor. He opened the curtains . . . and saw a big white figure walking through the apartment. Imagining that thieves had entered his room, he asked the white figure approaching his bed: "Who are you?" To which the specter solemnly replied: "I am the queen of heaven." The next day . . . he learned that the woman who had visited him was insane.

Toad

Toads have a special place in witchcraft. Witches are very fond of them, and pamper them as if they were children. They always take the precaution of having a few toads in their possession, and they train the toads to obey them. . . . Pierre Delancre says that the greatest witches are ordinarily attended by demons, and that these demons always sit on their left shoulder in the shape of a frog with two horns, but that they can be seen only by those who are practicing or who have practiced witchcraft.

Tower of Montpellier

There is in Montpellier an old tower believed by the local people to be the oldest in the world. Its fall is supposed to be followed in a few minutes by the destruction of the universe.

Tribunal of Westphalia

The secret tribunal of Westphalia . . . inspired such intense fear that people hardly dared pronounce its name. Charlemagne . . . is said to have sent an ambassador to Pope Leo III to ask what he should do about the rebels whom he could neither conquer nor exterminate. The Holy Father, after hearing the ambassador's words, arose without answering and went into his garden. There he gathered some brambles and bad herbs, fashioned a gibbet, and suspended from it the plants that he had gathered. The ambassador returned to Charlemagne and told him what he had seen. Charlemagne instituted the secret tribunal in Westphalia to force the pagans of the North to embrace Christianity and to weed out the nonbelievers. . . . Finally the tribunal was abolished by Emperor Maximilian I, at the beginning of the sixteenth century.

U

Ukobach

Demon belonging to a lower order. He always appears with an inflamed body. He is said to be the inventor of fireworks and the art of frying foods. Beelzebub has assigned to him the task of keeping oil in the infernal cauldrons.

Urine

Urine has admirable properties. It cures ringworm and ulcers in the ears if drunk as it is discharged by a healthy young man. It is also effective against the bite of serpents, asps and other poisonous reptiles. Witches apparently use it to make rain fall. Delrio reports that a peasant . . . was praising his daughter, aged eight, on account of the skill with which she performed her little function. "Oh, that's not all I can do," she replied. "I . . . can make it rain wherever you wish." She dug a hole in the ground, filled it with her urine, mixed in dirt, and uttered a few words. The rain came down in torrents. "Who taught you to do that?" shouted her astonished father. "My mother knows all about such things," she answered. The peasant . . . put his wife and his daughter on the wagon, took them to town, and turned them both over to the court.

Vampires

Name . . . given to men who have been dead for several years, or at least for several months, and who return, *body and soul,* talk, walk, defile villages, mistreat men and animals, suck the blood from their fellow men, exhaust them, and finally cause their death. The only way to free oneself from their dangerous visits . . . is to exhume them, impale them, cut off their heads, and tear out their hearts or burn them. Those who die after being sucked by them later become vampires. . . . Since their appetite keeps on increasing, they eat the cloth in which they are wrapped for burial. On leaving their graves at night, they go back to their relatives and friends, embrace them . . . and suck the blood from their necks. Their victims . . . soon die and become vampires, with the result that whole villages are infected. The only way . . . to break the cycle is to cut off the heads or pierce the hearts of the vampires.

Voltaire

Father Fiard numbers Voltaire among the demons incarnate, forerunners of the antichrist. He wrote treatises against vampires, apparitions, demons, and many other revered objects.

Werewolf or Lycanthrope

A man or woman transformed into a wolf through diabolical enchantment. . . . One day the citizens of Padua caught a werewolf that was running through the streets. They cut off his paws and he immediately regained the shape of a man, but had neither hands not feet, according to Fincel. Boguet . . . says that werewolves mate with she-wolves and enjoy mating with them as much as they enjoy intercourse with their wives. A distinctive trait of werewolves . . . is their predilection for fresh meat. Delancre states that they strangle dogs and children; that they enjoy their meals; that they walk on four feet; and that they bark like real wolves. . . . In Cervantes' last work, *Persiles y Sigismunda,* are lycanthropic islands and witches who change into she-wolves in order to abduct the men with whom they are in love. Every day a large number of unfortunate hypochondriacs, accused of lycanthropy, were burned, and theologians . . . complained because not enough of them were being destroyed.

Xaphan

Demon belonging to a lower order. When Satan and his angels revolted against God, Xaphan joined their ranks and was welcomed by them, for he had an inventive mind. He suggested that the rebels set fire to heaven, but he was hurled with the others to the bottom of the abyss, where he is forever engaged in fanning the embers in the furnaces. . . . He has as his emblem a pair of bellows.

Yan-Gant-Y-Tan

A demon who roams by night in Finistère. He carries five candles on his five fingers and can spin around as quickly as a reel. The people of Brittany think that the sight of Yan-Gant-Y-Tan is a bad omen.

Z

Zozo

Demon who, along with Mimi and Crapoulet, bewitched a young girl in the town of Teilly, in Picardy, in 1816. When she walked on all fours, Zozo was right behind her.

www.ingramcontent.com/pod-product-compliance
Lightning Source LLC
Chambersburg PA
CBHW032127090426
42743CB00007B/504